Teardrops & Gasoline

Madison Lauterborn

For information about special discounts for bulk purchases contact:
abigail@heartsunleashed.com

Manufactured in the United States of America
Library of Congress Cataloging-in-Publication Data Lauterborn, Madison.

Summary:

To exist is a gift disguised as a curse. We are given consciousness, but a lack of clarity. We are born curious, but encouraged to conform. The paradox of living ensures that to experience profound joy, we must also experience deep sorrow. These conflicting notions often culminate in a loss of identity accompanied by self-destructive tendencies. *Teardrops & Gasoline* is the poetic documentation of my personal journey from self-destruction to self-love; an artistic exploration of mental illness, traumatic experiences, versatile perspectives, recovery, and healing. This collection of poetry serves as a reminder that reality can be changed by choosing resilience.

ISBN:
978-1-968201-20-3 (paperback)
978-1-968201-26-5 (hardcover)

[1. Mental Health Poetry. 2. Healing and Recovery. 3. Self Love Journey.
4. Trauma and Resilience. 5. Emotional Healing Poetry. 6. Coming of Age
Poetry. 7. Spiritual Growth and Transformation]

The following book contains themes of mental illness, suicidal ideation,
self-harm, disordered eating, addiction, and sexual abuse.
Please read at your own discretion.

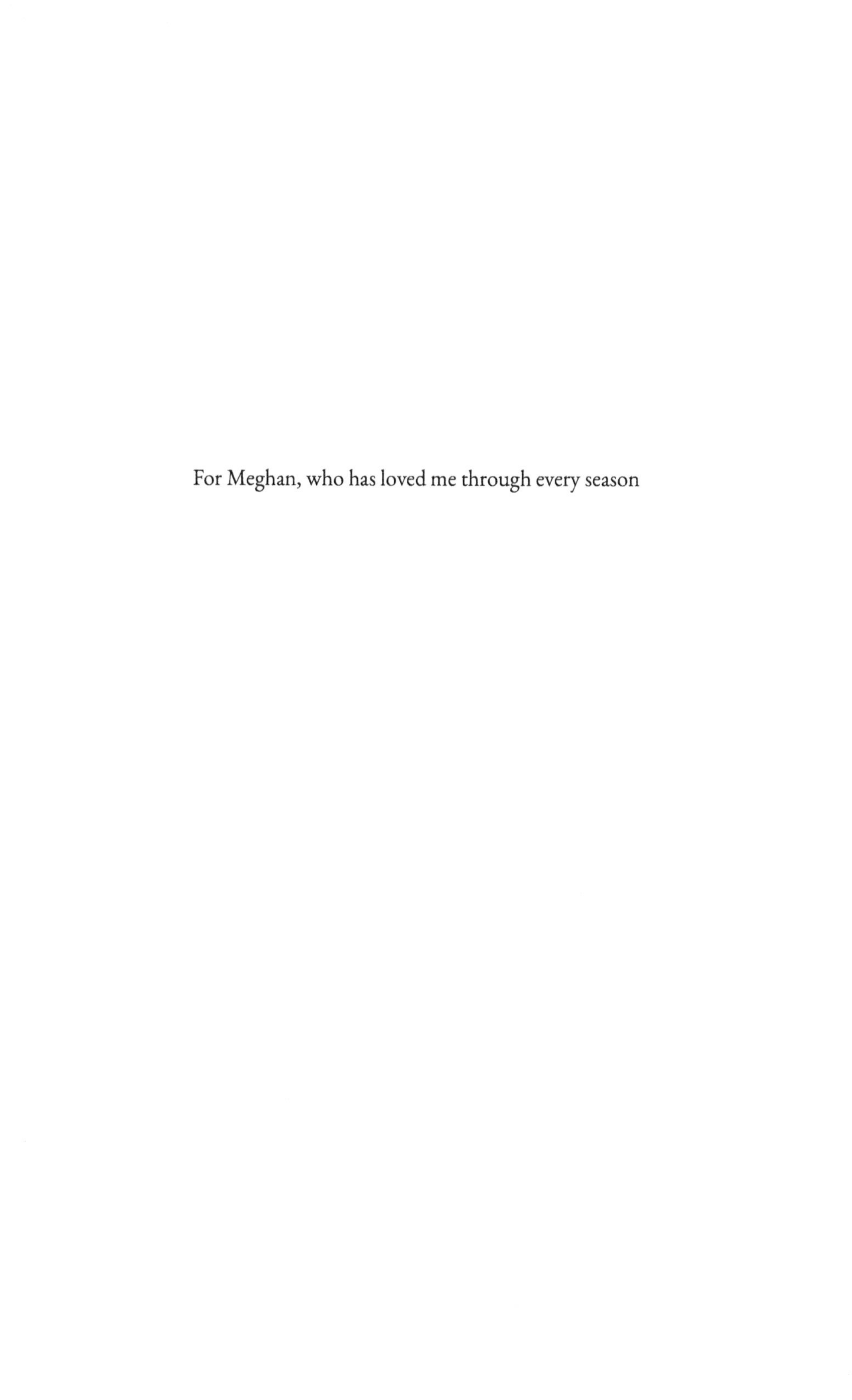

For Meghan, who has loved me through every season

I.
RAGE

Zoo

your arms were a cage
my cage
i was foolish enough to believe
that i had found salvation

little did i know
you held the key
and with it, the power
when i had taken refuge
you were plotting your escape

you left
and you locked me in
now i am trapped;
trapped within the cage
that binds my soul to you

Apologies

your lips taste bitter
as your calloused hands roam my body
and caress my scarred skin
you whisper promises in my ear
tell me lies
make me believe
every word that escapes your mouth
you are cruel,
unforgiving,
your apology burns
like the ghost of a palm on my cheek

Tattoos

crimson teardrops
the sting of a blade
sorrow masked by pain
pain masked by apathy
scars permanently
etched into my skin
like ink

Disguises

i wear a mask to hide who i am from you
i would rather disguise myself
than allow you to see
the damage that exists beneath

Apathetic Tendencies

i douse my emotions in bitter liquid
and quench my sorrows with liquor
my lips turn upward
as my throat ignites
fierce and misguided pleasure
transforms my expression
into a twisted smile
but i am not happy
i am not anything

when i look at you,
i finally feel nothing

Needle and Thread

you taught me the beauty
and devastation
of vulnerability

you unwound the fragile threads
that held my soul together
and promised that you were capable
of restoration

pieces of my heart
are now yours to keep
and i wonder,
do you know how to sew?

Pyromania

you reeked of desperation
and lust
your eyes communicated desire
and i knew
by the way our souls intertwined
that we would engulf one another in flames
it is a shame that you ran
fearful of a fire i ignited for you

The Snake

it is easier to blame you
to allow myself
the luxury of ignorance
make denial my new lover

reality is a snake
spitting venom into veins
setting fire to my chest
whispering poisonous words
in my ears

it is you
i still blame

Instruments

you carved a scar into my heart
with the knife that i handed you

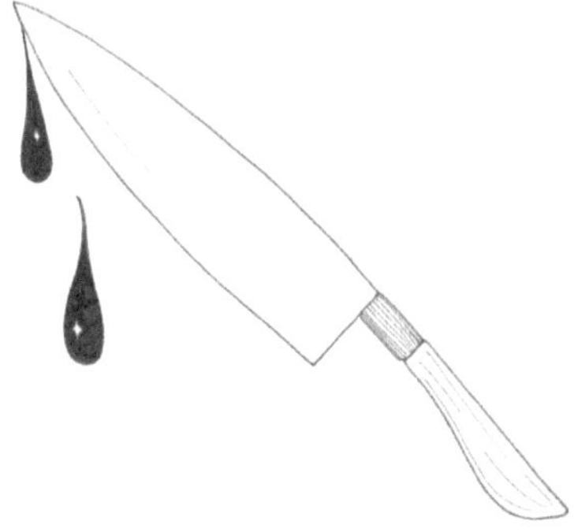

Table Prayer

i withhold from my body
everything needed to survive
and in my weakness that results,
i feel strong

what a sick form of nourishment

Table Prayer

i withhold from my body
everything needed to survive
and in my weakness that results,
i feel strong

Hunger

she does not use her teeth,
ignores her own mind,
instead she gorges herself
forgetting to breathe
between bites
she feels shame eat at her
as she tries to eat away
the shame
she does not realize
that she will never
feel full

Pages

i am afraid
that we do not exist

stories without endings
are not published

T

i'm an illusion
made up in your mind
when i speak my truth
you fix it with lies
your charming demeanor
a bullshit disguise
playing with fire
is your favorite vice

Wash

the conditioning that's occurred
has left no space for a fresh start
the pain is embedded in my bones,
etched into my skin,
a fabric woven into my mind
i know nothing of a life filled with joy
for i've left happiness behind

Angel

i do not believe

in guardian angels

they would have

warned me

about

you

The Way

the way you left
was the most painful
form of betrayal
your absence unexplained,
your reasoning unclear

the way you left
left me feeling
less than human

Definitions

you call it confidence
but what i see
is arrogance
driven by insecurity

J

i found myself apologizing
for mistakes that you made

Deepest Cut

allowing myself
to love you
scarred me deeper
than any blade
ever has

Teardrops and Gasoline

tears no longer
fall from my eyes
gasoline falls
drips
pours
down my cheeks

and you smile,
holding a match

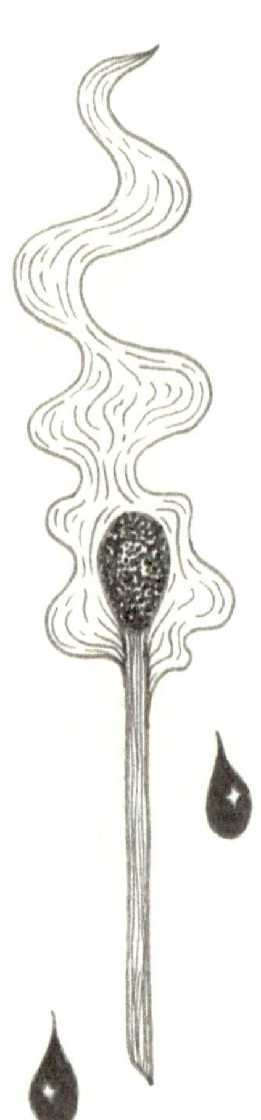

The Blues

every shade of blue
blended into one hue
could not match
the color of my soul

The Blues

every shade of blue
blended into one hue
could not match
the color of my soul

Unholy

consent was a word you hadn't learned yet
you were too young, too naive
you should have been too innocent
but you had a hunger for control
a desire for dominance that overpowered
any ounce of compassion within you
your roaming hands and reckless mouth
tainting my childhood with
unholy acts and unspoken truths
it is because of you that i learned to loathe
before i learned to love

Lost

i had entered
a realm of existence
so inexplicably dark
that i began confusing
pain with safety

Pottery

i covered my body with clay
and allowed the world to mold me
into any shape it desired
and when i looked at my reflection,
someone else stared back

The Question

if there is no feeling worse than this,
why do i revel in it?

The Answer

the pain has become so comfortable
that you've formed an attachment
to your own suffering

Origin of the Scars

my emotions awaken
the sorrow, anguish, resentment, shame
i feel them rising within me
threatening to overflow
like a flood

Stone Cold

i carved my face from marble
and it no longer betrayed my emotions

Codependence

turn my body into a cavern
of unrequited love and loss
i've found that i thrive on
chaos and codependence,
the illusion of your affection,
and promises on empty nights

self-awareness tells me i'm delusional
yet you seem like more than a vice
i apologize for my evasive disposition
but you don't seem to mind
for you are as broken as i am
and i am your kryptonite

Pride & Ego

i feel fulfilled in my own company
i need no validation to
know my own worth
if the world bowed to me
i'd walk in reverse

The Remedy

she replaces tears with scars
because pain is the only
remedy she knows

Sorrow

i am tired of waking every morning
wishing that i hadn't

Are You Okay?

her lips curl into a smile
as she nods her head reassuringly
the word *yes* rolls off her tongue
but inside she is screaming,
save me

Desperation

i am trapped
within my own mind,
tangled in a web of
fatalistic thoughts
and dark tendencies

Misery

not a cloud in the sky
but i still feel the rain

Fire and Ice

it begins as a flame
that becomes an inferno
transforming hope into ash
and teardrops into gasoline
it rages for days, weeks, months
engulfing the soul in a cloud of thick smoke
as vision is blurred by a crimson veil

and then hell freezes over
veins once burning with angst
suddenly laden with frost
it feels like relief
until the numbness sets in
its grip expanding across
layers of skin and layers of emotion
until there is no feeling
other than emptiness

and as the cycle continues,
an endless war between frost and flame,
you find yourself wondering which is worse
to feel everything
or nothing at all

Depression

it is a layer
of thick fog
that never vacates
the landscape

even when the sun shines,
it is masked by a haze

The Stage

my life is not mine
i view my reflection
and am met with
questions,
confusion,
uncertainty
i should have an oscar
the way i've denied authenticity
lived for others
loved for others
and nothing felt like me
i am no one
i am nothing
the person you know
is merely a reflection
of who you want me to be

Bandages

i found myself
by draining the blood
from my body
and healing the wounds
with apathy
and cheap liquor

Lust

feed my soul
with your violent hands
and hungry eyes

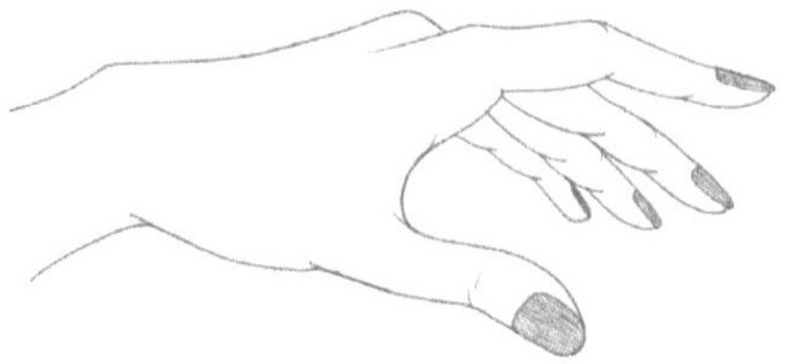

Vulnerability

i wonder if beneath my smile
you see the scars
the damage i try so hard to hide

if on my lips
you taste the bitterness
of a toxic past
and lovers who've left

if under my skin
you feel the ruins
the blackened ash of a broken soul

mostly,
i wonder if you
find yourself asking
why you are
with me at all

Pretty Things

they say there is beauty in the struggle
but these scars are anything but pretty

Hymn of the Broken

tidal waves
and lonely faces
spoken words
that time erases
empty graves
that reek of lust
shattered dreams
reduced to dust

Destruction

color my mind black and white
ebony, onyx, and shades of grey
cover my body with charcoal
and ignite me with your flames

Family Support

chaos swirls around me
like an autumn breeze
i feel the breath leave my lungs
as i drown beneath a sea
of your skepticism and doubt
i've run out of ways to please
you and your expectations
i can no longer breathe

Perception

i held onto the pain
like i held onto the bottle
welcoming the darkness
as it folded me in its embrace
and as i clothed my soul in black,
i felt toxic pleasure
flow through my veins,
convinced that there was
comfort in the chaos

Unsatisfied

lift a fork,
lose your dignity

Unsatisfied

lift a fork,
lose your dignity

Wings

she reeked of cigarettes and wine
and even though she stumbled
she felt as though
she could fly

Imperfections

soul full of whiskey, vodka, and gin
no forgiveness from the lord
i'm drowning in sin

33

and maybe my pain
stems from past experiences,
memories i've suppressed
and nights that i regret
but in this moment
when these emotions
overwhelm my body and mind
i no longer look to the past
for explanations or revelations,
i look only to self-destruction
hoping to find a cure
at the bottom of a pill bottle

Writer's Block

if my art comes from
the depths of my soul,
how can i write
when i feel as though
i've lost mine?

Unethical

and maybe i am alive
because of you,
but i would rather die
than thank you for the way
you took advantage
of my fragility

Swimsuit Season

i never liked bikinis
i could feel exposed in an oversized hoodie
and baggy sweatpants
a mask covering my smile, pair of sunglasses, and a baseball cap
it's funny, though
i once thought i liked attention
but i really just loved fooling people
i lived for the facade
carefully crafted personality, fluent in bullshit,
appearance perfectly curated for a specific audience
i was alluring but modest
an enticing mix of arrogance and insecurity
"the girl of my dreams," they'd say
and i ate it up as though it were my last meal
full, but never fully satisfied
because it wasn't attention i wanted
it was control
the illusion of exposure
without sharing my body
or bearing my soul
after all,
i never liked bikinis

The Starving Artist

someone asked me to describe
the future i saw for myself
and i stared at an empty canvas
still encased in flimsy plastic and layered with dust
strewn across the room were
empty paint canisters and soiled brushes
pages upon pages of torn up drawings littering the floor
ideas, i called them
ill conceived concepts of meaning and purpose
too big for one canvas or too small to hang on a wall
because the only commitment i never feared was stasis
the promise of a life unfulfilled
seemed more tangible than something worthwhile
so i guess when i think about the future
i see no future at all

Loneliness

treat your mind like a maze
puzzled and dazed
spend your days avoiding
yourself like the plague

Weather Patterns

my mind is always clouded
so i never mind the rain
drift further from myself
but feel grounded in the pain
find faith and fall from grace
just to waste another day
chasing versions of myself
that already lie in graves

Overconsumption

collecting empty thoughts
like food in the fridge
that we buy just to toss

Grey

behavioral patterns
pain masked by fake laughter
seeking the answers
fueling my own disasters
lifestyle, bad habits
undeniably tragic
everything's madness
i fade into static

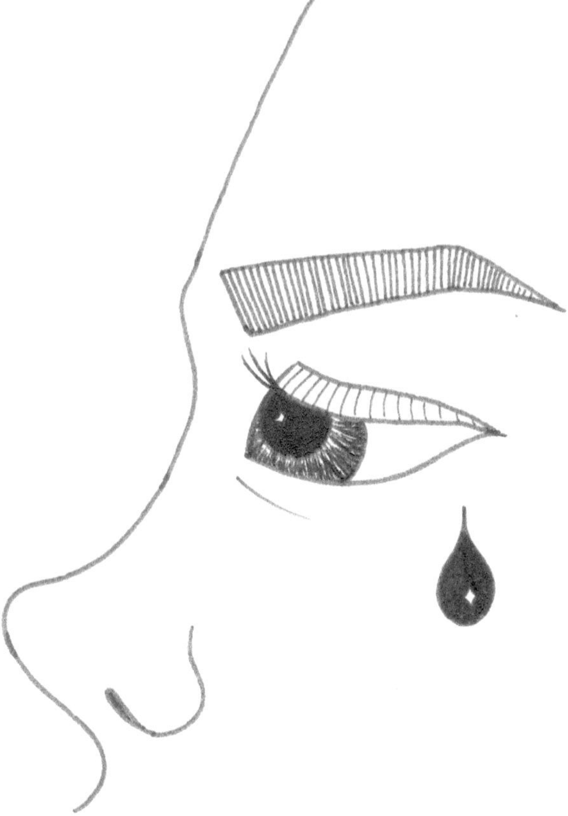

Hopeless

even in the moment
it feels like a memory
there's no hope for us
when life's never felt real to me

Drunk in Lust

underneath a neon sky
i captured your heart
and you captured my mind
the stars danced
as our hands intertwined
hard to ignore
this lust at first sight
i long to know you,
feel your lips on mine
drowning in liquor
but i'm drunk on your vibe

II.
RESILIENCE

Worship

if the body is a temple,
i've been neglecting my religion

Grief

i have grieved the death
of my old identity
and welcomed the birth
of a new perspective
with arms wider than
the expanse of the ocean

Inspiration

when the fog lifted
the sky smiled at me
i danced in the forest and sang to the moon
as the stars told me stories
of the girl who once walked within shadows,
safe from the secrets they kept
she went to the river to beg for forgiveness
and the atmosphere wept, saying,
"if you wish to receive, you must be willing to accept"

On the Wall

her eyes trace her reflection
endlessly searching
for the girl she once was
she has forgotten how fast
reflections change

Toxicity

there are still moments
when i find myself wondering
how i could have changed
to please you
it is for this reason
i know you are
toxic

Perseverance

i will smile,

laugh,

persevere

until my cheeks grow sore

until my throat aches

until i have healed

and these pages

will be the only evidence

that i was ever weak

1:36 am

the clock tells lies
speaks the language of a new day
of a new morning

i have yet to fall asleep

Coping Mechanisms

it cannot be called coping
if it harms
more than it heals

Evening Lullaby

the sky is dark like my aura
but your eyes light up the night
as if they are composed of
thousands of constellations,
collapsing into themselves and
radiating warmth throughout my bones,
throughout my soul
you make life meaningful
with just one glance

Seasons

she was like a
tree in autumn,
prepared for death
but capable of restoration

Chains

i feared letting go
of the pain and suffering
i feared losing myself
in recovery
and silencing my voice
through healing
i failed to realize
that i had already
lost myself
by holding onto
what was destroying me

Turn Pain Into Art

i painted canvases
with my blood
and cleansed the brushes
with my tears

Desires

the symmetry of life
bores me
give me abstract
give me substance
i want to feel deeply
and passionately
i want experiences
that surpass the realm
of understanding
that ignite curiosity
and nourish the soul
i want more than
simply existence
i want meaning
i want purpose
i want direction

Dinner for Two

i poured my soul
into your glass
placed my emotions
on a silver platter
and fed you memories
of my past

Conflicted

what a wicked tragedy it is
to crave both recovery and relapse

Contemplation

i went to the woods
to contemplate existence
and found great comfort
in painful introspection

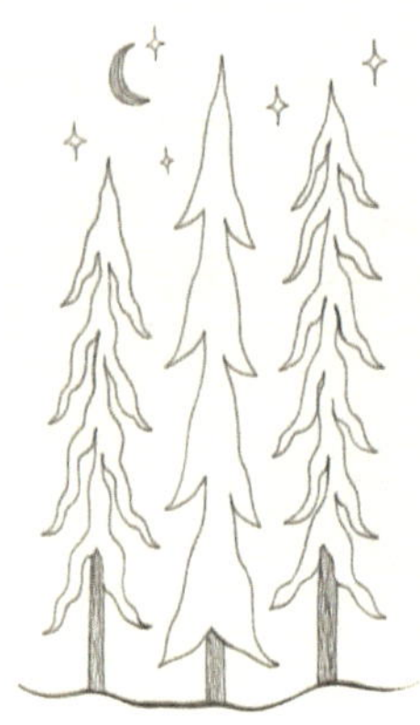

Are You Happy?

i think happy is the wrong word
it's too broad,
overused,
widely misunderstood
i'm not unhappy
but i'm not content
you see, i'm proud of the progress i've made
of the person i'm becoming
but that doesn't negate the suffering i've endured
the experiences i've survived
so i wouldn't say that i'm happy
but i am finally finding peace

Silence

in the solitude of my own thoughts
the loneliness transformed
and it wasn't because
i felt understood by the world
but because i finally began
to understand myself

Independence

i realized my own strength
when i no longer ran from
the uncomfortable or unfamiliar,
but fully embraced the storm
and accepted the aftermath,
it was when i recognized
my responsibility for growth
that i discovered independence

Genesis

pain cannot be silenced
until the body recognizes
the fuel that feeds the fire

Saving Grace

writing saved me from myself
words became bandages
as ink cauterized my wounds
the blood, the tears, the trials
ceased when i put pen to paper

Preserver

you don't need to wait
until you're drowning
to ask for a lifejacket

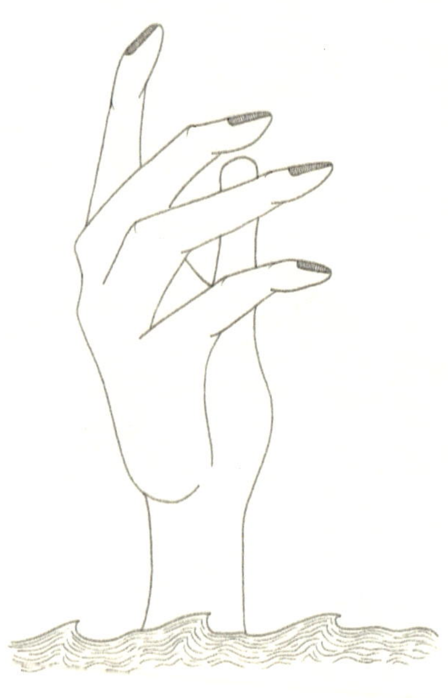

Runaway

i want to run into the sunset
and escape from my past
paint myself a new image
then never look back

Hard Truth

when pain is more familiar than peace,
self destruction feels like safety

Hard Truth

when pain is more familiar than peace,
self destruction feels like safety

Alcoholism

it's difficult to believe that i lived the way i did
the unimaginable horrors and sleepless nights seem far away now
foggy memories and fleeting feelings waiting to be forgotten
but i don't think i'll ever forget, not really
not when it altered the trajectory of my life
brought me down paths i never intended to walk
pushed me so close to the edge it felt as though i'd already fallen
no, i don't think i'll ever forget
and i don't think i want to
for the past is a testament to my resilience
a representation of all i've overcome
a haunting reminder of who i once was
my motivation for moving forward

Misconstrued Notions

when you identify too deeply with
a traumatic event,
a diagnosis,
a behavioral pattern,
you deny yourself the ability to heal effectively
you make suffering a personality trait
rather than an experience
to learn from,
to grow from,
to heal from

III.
RECOVERY

Melodies

if i were to write music
with what i feel for you,
every song would be
a different genre

Mother

your love kept me alive
it was enough
to be shared between
the two of us
and multiplied
in your arms,
i survived

Us

it was not love at first
it was friendship
mixed with curiosity

Distance

there's something spiritual about the space
between thoughts and words
you see, the mind is a sacred place
where dreams remain hidden
inspiration untouched
true feelings tucked into corners
that feel cozy, but keep us closed off
it isn't until the heart decides
to unveil what the mind has conjured up
and turn it into conversation
that we find ourselves at the precipice
of something supernatural
in the space between
a realm where vulnerability and courage intertwine
where thoughts and words become one
as minds converge amidst the mingling of souls

Passion

striking landscapes
and silenced time
vivid hues painted
across folds of my mind
foreign emotions
every time that we grind
passion rains when i know
that you're mine

Self-Compassion

you are resilient and beautiful
with an intellectual mind
and depth greater than the ocean
the universe exists within you
stars,
planets,
galaxies
orbiting every fiber of your being
and the very essence of your soul
you are exquisite,
a work of art

you must learn to love yourself
for all that you are
and all that you'll become

Complexities

the connection between mind and body
never ceases to amaze me,
my mind recognizes that when
your eyes pour into mine
you are simply glancing,
but my body responds as though
you have performed
a symphony within me

Recovery

it will feel earth shattering,
as if every atom in your body
has been ignited
and charged with electricity
you will experience grief, sorrow, agony
but also hope, love, and serenity
it will exhaust you in ways
you never knew possible
but believe me when i say
it is worth it

Purpose

you would not exist
if you weren't meant to

Mind Over Matter

i feel your energy from across the room
our eyes do not meet
but our thoughts intertwine
emotions unravel the threads
that separate us
and passion ignites a flame
that fuses our bones
you undress me with your mind
and touch me with your soul

At First Sight

my veins burn
with the thought
of wanting you

Flight

another universe exists
above the clouds
a serene and tranquil
escape from reality
where thoughts become dreams
and fear becomes flight

Contentment

the empty canvas
that was once my mind
is slowly transforming
into a work of art
a brilliant display
of hues foreign to me
colorful representations
of the person i've waited
so long to be

Royalty

nose ring and tight jeans
i've never felt like a queen
but with you
i could conquer anything

Him

he has me
feeling like a child
with a crush
for the first time

Time Machine

i once feared the future
but found myself living in the past
and when the past caused me pain
i ran into the distance,
seeking asylum in the unknown

it wasn't until i realized
that it is here and now
where we find peace
that i discovered my own

Bloom

i looked at my reflection
and saw not fear
but blind acceptance

Blessed

these eyes have granted me sight
but this mind has granted me vision

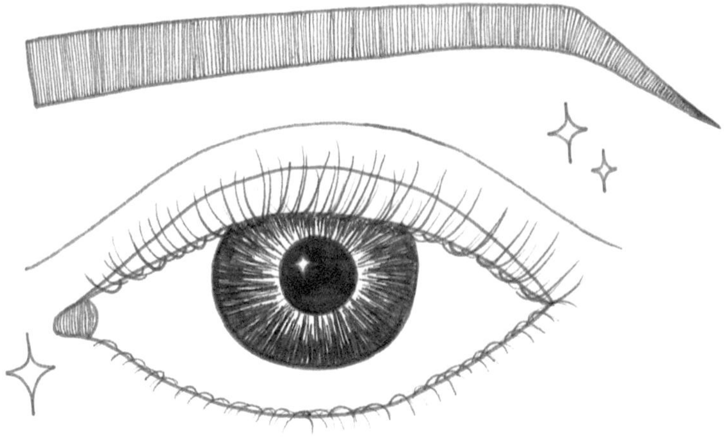

Floral Arrangement

and like a rose,
you bloom with uncertainty
but even thorns
cannot mask your beauty
you attempt to portray
an exterior of strength
and still you emanate softness

Andromeda

when i was empty
you were my remedy
i drowned in a galaxy
composed of your energy

Changes

challenge your thoughts, change your feelings
change your feelings, broaden your perspective
broaden your perspective, enhance your life

Show and Tell

show me the world through your lens
and i'll paint heaven in your eyes
you take me somewhere foreign to my mind
entice me with words
that sink into my bones
like weight into water
drown me in your river
and cleanse my soul with your radiance
take my hand as we travel the universe
let the stars guide your heart to mine

S

the way he opens my legs and expands my mind
feels like shakespeare writing in a different time
his voice is like honey
soft but rich with excitement
his past a blend of pain and passion
his present beaming with brightness
a future fueled by ambition
the promise of abundance
life with him looks like stardust and comets
he has the mind of a philosopher
quick wit like a comic
an energy so strong
it'd be a shame not to flaunt it
minutes turn into hours
and if i'm being honest
the way that i've fallen
has forever written on it

Mural

you've been treated like a child's illustration
a sketch made with crayon on a post-it note,
hung carelessly on the fridge to be forgotten
but you, my dear
you are divine
a complex composition of colors,
patterns,
textures,
and lines
art galleries can't hold you
the poets can't rhyme
you silence the stars
when it's your time to shine

Meditation

darkness descends behind my eyes
as i slip into a sea of tranquility and peace
there is no fear in this darkness
for i become the light
i unzip my skin and step into the void
my soul its own galaxy,
illuminated by divine thoughts
as i dance through time
to the hum of my heartbeat
and the rhythm of my lungs

Rejuvenation

i swam in the depths of my subconscious
and found clarity within the abyss
compassion replaced criticism
empathy eradicated envy
strength outweighed sorrow
i became the instrument
of my rejuvenation
and learned to wade in the waters
rather than wallow or drown

Growing Pains

growth often hurts before it heals
like a bone stretching with age
or a scar just beginning to fade
many shy away from the discomfort
finding solace in pills, booze, places, people
delaying growth with ignorance and inaction
but in order to heal
to truly unmask the trauma of the past
we must embrace the growing pains
learn to love the person in the mirror
master the art of acceptance
and allow forgiveness to flow freely
it is through surrender
through faith in the process
that we find strength

The Let Down

if a connection no longer serves you
no longer allows you the space to evolve
or grow into yourself without inducing guilt,
letting go may be kinder than
salvaging something that cannot be saved,
choosing yourself over unstable relationships
is often difficult but necessary
what at first feels painful
will ultimately bring peace

Bliss

i find clarity in the stillness of quiet mornings
the pitter patter of footsteps on cool wooden floors,
the warmth of my lover's body pressed against mine,
whispers of daylight dancing through drawn curtains
my life was once defined by restless evenings,
the overconsumption of low vibrations,
and a different couch every night
this was the soundtrack i played on repeat
until i found peace in new genres
the bliss of routine
with the man that i love
and a soul that's now clean

Wisdom

the knowledge that we know nothing
is the greatest form of clarity
wisdom is derived from the
acceptance of our own ignorance
and the passionate desire
to improve upon it

Real Love

i crave a love that is challenging, but not painful
a relationship founded on loyalty without attachment
intimacy inspired by attraction, not lust
a connection sustained through aligned values, never avoidance

Textures

life will attempt to harden you
to turn passion into pessimism,
hope into hate,
appreciation into anger,
but i refuse to resort to cruelty
to allow discordant notes
to string together a ballad of rage or iniquity
you see, i've spent too much of my life
feeling angry, afraid, insecure
now, i seek only peace
the serenity that stems from stillness
i surround myself with energy
that reflects light and warmth
because the world may view softness as weakness,
but i transform that weakness into strength

Secret Garden

your mind is a garden
so tend to the wildflowers,
pay no mind to the weeds
water the things that sprout joy,
don't plant poisonous seeds

Mahogany

when a relationship fades,
it's important to allow the memories
to contribute color to the canvas of your life
without letting them distort the entire image,
the picture you began painting
before their entry into your existence
must still be completed,
there are simply different colors now

Mother Part Two

you remind me of the budding trees during spring
the wildflowers peaking through overgrown brush
a full moon on an overcast evening
you've taught me the art of acceptance
of overcoming adversity
you've shown me the power of independence
of love, life, and meaning

The Art of Letting Go

"but how do you let go of the pain?" she asked,
her inquisitive eyes full of sadness
"by doing it over and over again," i replied
like any great form of art,
it requires practice

The Exception

in psychology, it is said
that the intensity of any emotion
can last for only a brief time
before excitement fades,
before sorrow dissipates,
before disappointment subsides,
but i've found that there are exceptions to this rule
they are love and gratitude
with subtle beginnings
that become profoundly expansive
these feelings grow without limits
become things we can't define,
the only requirements are
nurture and consistency

Whatever Happens

i recognize the importance of planning
of forming goals, having dreams
but i surrender my attachment
to a future that isn't promised
i long to be fluid, adaptable
to be so committed to gratitude and growth
that even disappointments feel like blessings
like redirections that guide me to where i'm meant to be

Acknowledgements

A sincere thanks to my dearest friends—Meghan, Bailey, and Jordan—who have chosen to love every version of me through every chapter of life thus far.

Mom, I wouldn't have lived to share this collection of poetry with the world if not for your unconditional love, compassion, patience, and encouragement. Having you as a mother is the most precious gift I've been blessed with in this life. My appreciation for you is beyond words.

Jeff, I am so grateful for our relationship. I can't thank you enough for always seeing the greatness in me and for challenging me to persevere.

Dad and Jubilee, thank you for teaching me the value of connection, responsibility, and integrity.

Shaelamar, my love, the gratitude I feel for you is endless. Thank you for loving me for who I've been, who I am, and who I'm becoming. I'm incredibly thankful for the support and love that you provide me with, for the laughter and joy that we share, and for the acceptance and inspiration you offer.

Melanie, thank you for helping me discover the joy of sober living, the power of surrender, and the beauty of healing. So much of my success is a direct result of your presence in my life.

To Abigail and the entire Hearts Unleashed team, thank you for making this dream of mine a reality. I sincerely appreciate the time and dedication that has gone into every step of this journey.

Author Bio

Madison Lauterborn is a writer and artist based in Appleton, Wisconsin. Her work is inspired by her lived experiences, spirituality, and her dedication to growth and healing. *Teardrops & Gasoline* is her first published work, and she intends to continue writing and creating artwork that reflects the complexities of the human experience. You can follow her journey on instagram @madisonlauterborn and @mad.lau